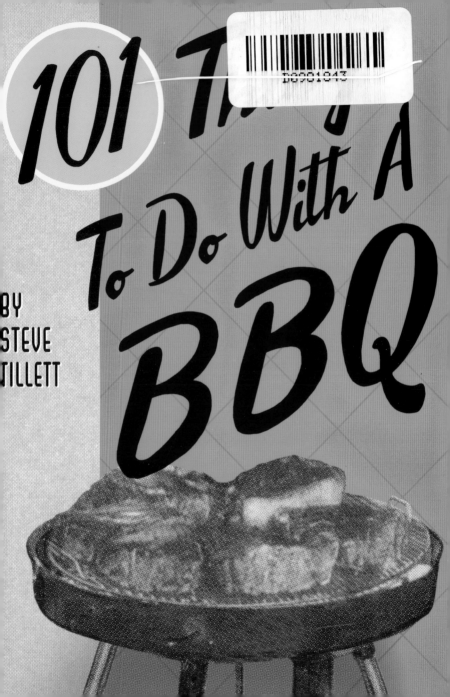

101 Things To Do With A BBQ

BY STEVE TILLETT

101 Things To Do With A BBQ

101 Things To Do With A BBQ

BY
STEVE TILLETT

Gibbs Smith, Publisher
Salt Lake City

This book is dedicated to Suzanne Taylor, whose vision helped bring this book to fruition, and to my father the butcher, who taught me to BBQ and has always inspired me to accomplish anything I want to achieve. Also, to my beautiful wife and best friend, Sharon (queen of the kitchen), and to my children Chris, Andie, Kittie, and Matthew, who have survived my many BBQ experiments, and are still willing to be my honorable taste testers. And finally, to my friends Stephanie Lamberson, Tiffany Felt, Jennifer Waldrip, the salmon king Jeff Tillett, G-ma Tillett, Grandma Barbara Gibbs, my little friend Coach Solomona Tapasa, Janice Horschel, Jennifer Pfleiger, and others who contributed their favorite family recipes to this collection. A special thanks to Jeff Tillett for designing our fabulous BBQ website: www.bbq101.com.

First Edition
09 08 07 06 05   20 19 18 17 16 15 14 13 12 11 10 9 8 7 6 5 4 3

Published by
Gibbs Smith, Publisher
P.O. Box 667
Layton, Utah 84041

Orders: 1.800.748.5439
www.gibbs-smith.com

Consulting editor: Stephanie Ashcraft
Designed by Kurt Wahlner
Printed and bound in Korea

Library of Congress Cataloging-in-Publication Data

Tillett, Steve.
  101 things to do with a BBQ / Steve Tillett.—1st ed.
     p. cm.
  ISBN 1-58685-698-7
  1. Barbecue cookery. I. Title.

TX840.B3T554 2005
641.5'784—dc22   2004021117

CONTENTS

Poultry

Simplest BBQ Chicken 66 • Melissa's Jazzed-Up BBQ Chicken 67 • Scott's Tantalizing Dry Rub Chicken—On a Can 68 • Smoked Honey Garlic BBQ Chicken 69 • Smoky Mopped Chicken 70 • Morris's Alabama-style BBQ Chicken 71 • Grandma's BBQ Cola Chicken 72 • Janice's Tangy Chicken 73 • Tapasa's Samoan-Style Chicken 74 • Island Grilled Teriyaki Chicken 75 • Tap's Succulent Chicken 76 • Jen's Egyptian Grilled Chicken 77 • Stuffed Chicken Breast 78 • Bacon-Stuffed Chicken Breast 79 • Crabby Stuffed Chicken Breast 80 • Orange Sesame Chicken 81 • Grilled Chili Sauce Chicken 82 • Italian Chicken 83 • Grant's Monday-Night-Special Buffalo Wings 84 • Jazzy BBQ Turkey Legs 85 • Smoked Honey Garlic BBQ Turkey 86

Pork

Rockin' Chops 88 • Jazzed-Up BBQ Pork Steaks 89 • Dry Rub Pork Chops 90 • Perfect Rubbed Ribs 91 • Dry Rub Pulled Pork 92 • Smoked Honey Garlic BBQ Pork 93 • Smoked & Mopped Pulled Pork 94 • Floyd's Doctored-Up Pork Steaks 95 • Cilantro Pork Steak 96 • Chris's Kickin' Mustard Ribs 97 • Grilled Pork Citrus Steaks 98 • Spicy Rubbed Pork Roast 99 • Orange Salsa Ribs 100

Seafood

Sharon's Super Salmon 102 • My Big Bro's Salmon Foil Specialty 103 • J.W.'s Cedar Plank Salmon with Brown Sugar Rub 104 • Bacon-Wrapped Shrimp 105 • Basil Shrimp 106 • Simple White Fish 107 • Grilled Parmesan Halibut 108 • Lemon Cilantro Fish Steaks 109 • Crab-Stuffed Mushrooms 110 • Creamy Crab-Stuffed Mushrooms 111

Desserts

Grilled Apple Delight 114 • Perfect Pears 114 • Ryan's Tasty Banana Treats 115 • Just Peachie 116 • Chocolate Banana Bang-a-rang 117 • Banana Dream Boat 118 • Could it be Cantaloupe 118 • Sweet BBQ Pineapple 119 • Katherine's Snail Snacks 120

Bonus Section: Sauces and Rubs

Jazzed-Up BBQ Sauce 122 • Steve's Famous Dry Rub 122 • Four-Minute BBQ Sauce 122 • Honey Garlic BBQ Sauce 123 • Mop Sauce 123 • Big Red's Spicy Dry Rub 123 • Alabama White BBQ Sauce 124 • Brine 124 • Sauce from Scratch 124 • Floyd's Fantastic Sauce 125 • Coach's Island-Style Marinade 125 • Texas BBQ Sauce 126 • Hawaiian Ginger Marinade 126

HELPFUL HINTS

1. Turn meat with tongs instead of a fork so you don't puncture the meat and let out the natural juices.

2. It is best to baste on the BBQ during the last 5 minutes of grilling. BBQ sauce burns easily, so this method will help to avoid scorching any type of marinade or sauce.

3. Boil leftover marinade in a saucepan over high heat. This kills any bacteria left by raw meat and makes it safe to use for basting during the last 5 minutes of grilling, or as a warm sauce for the finished dish.

4. Liquid smoke used in small amounts is a great way to make your food taste like it spent all day in the smoker.

5. When using aluminum foil to cover food, put food on the shiny side. If the shiny side is facing out, it will reflect heat and slow cooking.

6. Smoking foods on a gas grill is easy. The only things needed are wood chips and a smoker box. Pick up "smoker" wood chips from a local sporting goods store. Apple, cherry, hickory, or mesquite chips work well for pork, beef, or poultry. Try alder for any fish.

7. If you don't own a smoker box or don't want to buy one, they are easy to make. Follow these simple instructions:

Tear off a piece of heavy-duty aluminum foil, 12 inches long. Place wood chips in the middle and wrap securely. Poke holes in top of pouch with a meat thermometer and it's ready to go. For large cuts of meat like roasts, place the wood chips in water and soak 30 minutes to 2 hours, then place wood chips in smoker box. For smaller cuts of meat, dry chips are fine. Place your smoker box under the grilling grate, directly over the flame. Turn grill to high heat until smoke begins to rise from pouch. Immediately turn grill down to desired cooking temperature. Cook your food on the appropriate temperature and let the wood chips go to work.

8. Meat is always more tender when cooked at a low temperature, no matter how high the grade. Also, meat served hot is usually more tender than meat served cold.

9. As a general rule, use approximately 1 1/2 cups of marinade for every 1 to 2 pounds of meat. Make sure it completely covers the meat. Let your meat marinate in a zipper-lock plastic bag in the refrigerator. Double-bag to prevent leaks. You can also freeze marinating meats for future uses.

10. Marinade is the quickest way to tenderize meat and add additional flavor. A quick 30-minute marinate will give meat a great flavor. Marinating even longer will give you more flavor. When marinating in the refrigerator, remove meat and let it come to room temperature before grilling.

11. Spray the grill with cooking spray, or wipe it down with oil prior to grilling to prevent your food from sticking. This will also make it easier to clean the grill once you're done grilling.

12. To clean the grill after using, lay a piece of foil over the grill, shiny side down, and turn to high heat for 5 minutes. This will burn off any buildup on the grill. Watch the grill closely, don't walk away. When the 5 minutes is up, gently brush grill with a wire brush.

13. For a grill that needs some serious cleaning, try using 2 tablespoons baking soda added to 1 cup water. Brush it on with your wire brush. Let sit for 2-3 minutes, then scrub with the wire brush.

ADVANCED GRILLING TIPS

Beef: fillet mignon, steaks, ribs, roasts, etc.

1. Cook beef according to taste as times show below.

Thickness	Doneness	Grilling Time (total)
1 inch	rare	6 minutes
	medium	10 minutes
1 1/2 inches	rare	10–12 minutes
	medium	15–18 minutes
2 inches	rare	15 minutes
	medium	20 minutes

2. Cook roast according to taste as times and temperatures show below.

Rare	Medium	Well
140 degrees	160 degrees	170 degrees
20 minutes per pound	25 minutes per pound	30 minutes per pound

3. To BBQ, turn grill to high heat. The hotter the grill, the better it will seal in the juices. Place beef on grill and sear 1 minute on each side, using tongs to turn it so the natural juices stay sealed. Then turn grill down to medium heat and finish grilling according to taste and desired doneness. Turn several times throughout total grilling time.

Poultry: chicken, turkey, etc.

1. The trick to grilling chicken is to do it slowly and turn it frequently. Approximate cooking time is 20–30 minutes for chicken breasts, tenders, or thighs, and 20 minutes per pound if chicken is whole.

2. When cooking chicken with skin on, put a layer of foil on the bottom rack of the grill, and cook the chicken on the middle or top rack. This will reduce the flare-ups and decrease the chance of burning.

3. To check if chicken is cooked through, squeeze it. When the juices run clear it is probably done. Double-check by slicing open one of the bigger pieces when you think it is done.

4. To thaw frozen chicken, remove from freezer and place in the refrigerator the day before use. If in a hurry or for same-day use, place chicken in a bowl and fill with cool water. Allow to soak until thawed. Change water every few minutes to speed up the process.

Pork:

1. Pork is naturally drier than other meats. Do not to overcook it. Approximate cooking time is 30–35 minutes per pound.

2. Marinades and brines will add a lot of flavor while helping to moisten your pork.

Seafood:

1. When grilling fish, do not turn it, and quickly remove it from grill when it is no longer opaque. Do not overcook.

2. Leave scales on bigger fish and cook scale side down. Salmon on the grill is best cooked in foil.

3. Grill trout over direct heat to add a hearty smoked flavor.

4. Other fish like swordfish, tuna, mackerel, and bluefish are great choices for grilling because their natural oils help keep them moist and flaky.

5. Thicker fillets stand up to the heat of the grill better than thin ones.

APPETIZERS

STEPHANIE'S FRESH GRILLED VEGETABLES

combination of cherry tomatoes, asparagus, zucchini, and **sweet bell peppers**
$^1/_4$ cup **olive oil** (adjust as needed)
salt and pepper, to taste

Preheat grill to medium-high heat. Clean and cut all vegetables except asparagus into $^1/_4$- to $^1/_2$-inch-thick slices or wedges. Sprinkle olive oil over top. Turn grill to low heat and place vegetables on rack.* Grill 2–3 minutes and turn over. Grill 2–3 minutes more, then season with salt and pepper. Serve with ranch dressing for dipping. Makes 3–5 servings.

*If the vegetables are small enough to fall through the grate, you can use a frying pan right on the grill instead.

POPPIN' BBQ POPCORN

¹/₄ cup **popcorn kernels**
¹/₈ cup **vegetable oil**
1 to 2 tablespoons **butter,** melted
Steve's Famous Dry Rub (see Sauces
and Rubs, page 122)

Preheat grill to high heat. Cover bottom of a large and deep saucepan
(with ovenproof handles) with a single layer of popcorn kernels. Pour
oil over top of kernels. Place saucepan, covered, on grill over high heat
until the popcorn begins to pop. Start to gently shake the pan, continu-
ing until popcorn is completely popped, about 3–6 minutes. Transfer
to a serving bowl and drizzle popcorn with melted butter, stirring as
you drizzle. Sprinkle desired amount of dry rub over popcorn and stir
again to mix well. Makes 3–5 cups popped popcorn.

GRILLED PARMESAN
POTATO SLICES

4 **medium potatoes**
4 tablespoons **grated Parmesan cheese**
salt and pepper or **seasoning salt,** to taste

Preheat grill to medium heat. Cut potatoes lengthwise into $1/4$-inch strips, then place in a large bowl. Sprinkle Parmesan cheese and seasoning over top. Using tongs, place potatoes on grill and turn every 4–6 minutes; cook 12–18 minutes, or until done. Serve with ranch dressing or other sauces for dipping. Makes 3–5 servings.

STUFFED TOMATOES

4 to 6	**medium** or **large tomatoes**
2 cups	**crushed croutons**
1 cup	**finely chopped sweet onion**
1 tablespoon	**minced garlic**
1 tablespoon	**finely chopped cilantro**
	salt and pepper, to taste

Preheat grill to medium heat. Partially core tomatoes. Mix croutons, sweet onion, garlic, and cilantro in a bowl. Scoop and pack mixture into hollowed centers of tomatoes. Place tomatoes on grill 10 minutes. Season with salt and pepper. Makes 3–5 servings.

BLUE CHEESE-STUFFED MUSHROOMS

I pound **fresh mushrooms,** stems removed
5 ounces **blue cheese** or **feta**
$^1/_4$ cup **olive oil**

Fill mushroom caps with crumbled cheese. Preheat grill to medium-high heat, and lightly oil grate. Place mushrooms, cheese side up, onto grill. Do not turn mushrooms over. Just grill until cheese melts and mushrooms are tender. Makes 4–6 servings.

VARIATION: For added flavor, top with grilled onions (see page 30).

GRILLED STUFFED PEPPERS

4 to 6	**medium** or **large sweet bell peppers,** any color
1 1/2 cups	**crushed croutons**
1 cup	**finely chopped sweet onion**
1/2 cup	**grated Parmesan cheese**
1 tablespoon	**minced garlic**
1 tablespoon	**finely chopped cilantro**
	salt and pepper, to taste

Preheat grill to medium heat. Clean and core peppers. Mix croutons, sweet onion, Parmesan cheese, garlic, and cilantro in a bowl. Scoop and pack mixture into hollowed centers of peppers. Place peppers on grill 15 minutes. Season with salt and pepper. Makes 4–6 servings.

AVIATOR'S GRILLED CAESAR SALAD

6 cups	**torn romaine lettuce**
I cup	**sliced cucumber**
2	**medium Roma tomatoes,** cut into wedges
3 tablespoons	**grated Parmesan cheese**
I bottle	**Caesar salad dressing**
	freshly ground pepper, to taste

Toppings (choose I or more):

        grilled chicken breasts, cubed
        grilled shrimp
        croutons

Evenly divide all ingredients except dressing onto individual serving plates. Serve with dressing on the side. Makes 2–4 servings.

TIFFANY'S CUBAN POTATOES

3 pounds	**potatoes** (sweet and Yukon are good here)
2 to 3 tablespoons	**olive oil**
	salt and pepper, to taste
3 to 4	**garlic cloves,** minced
1 to 3 tablespoons	**fresh lime juice**
1 1/2 tablespoons	**chopped fresh parsley**

Preheat grill to medium-high heat. Slice potatoes lengthwise into $^1/_4$- to $^1/_8$-inch-thick slices. Toss potatoes in bowl with olive oil and season with salt and pepper. Grill until tender, about 20–30 minutes. Cool on a wire rack 15 minutes. Transfer to a large bowl and toss with garlic, lime juice, and parsley. If potatoes appear dry, add more olive oil and season with salt and pepper again. Makes 4–6 servings.

VEGETABLES

TROY'S SPICY ITALIAN VEGGIES

**combination of Roma tomatoes, onions,
yellow squash,** and **green bell peppers**
$^1/_4$ cup **Italian salad dressing** (adjust as needed)
2 teaspoons **basil**
salt and pepper, to taste

Preheat grill to medium-high heat. Cut all vegetables into $^1/_4$- to
$^1/_2$-inch-thick slices or wedges. Brush with Italian dressing. Sprinkle
with basil, salt, and pepper. Grill cut side up 4–6 minutes, or until
heated through. Do not turn. Grill vegetables directly on the rack
or use a frying pan on the grill. Makes 3–5 servings.

VARIATION: For an even spicier version, marinate vegetables in dressing
for up to 6 hours.

GRILLED BUTTER AND GARLIC VEGETABLES

combination of asparagus, yellow squash, patty pan, mushrooms, and **red bell peppers**
4 tablespoons **melted butter** (adjust as needed)
1 teaspoon **minced garlic**
seasoning salt or **salt and pepper,** to taste

Preheat grill to medium-high heat. Cut all vegetables except asparagus into $1/4$- to $1/2$-inch-thick slices or wedges and place in a large bowl. Combine the melted butter and garlic, then pour over the vegetables and toss. Grill 4 minutes or until heated through, turning at 1-minute intervals. Grill vegetables directly on the rack or use a frying pan on the grill. Serve with seasoning salt or salt and pepper. Makes 3–5 servings.

GRILLED LEMON VEGETABLES

combination of zucchini, yellow squash, and **purple onions**
1/4 cup **olive oil** (adjust as needed)
2 teaspoons **dried chopped onion**
1 teaspoon **lemon juice**
salt and pepper, to taste

Preheat grill to medium-high heat. Cut all vegetables into 1/4- to 1/2-inch-thick slices or wedges. Combine oil, onion, and lemon juice. Place vegetables in a bowl, pour mixture over top, and toss. Turn BBQ down to medium-low heat and place vegetables directly on the grill.* Grill 4–6 minutes, turning every minute until tender. Serve hot with salt and pepper. Makes 3–5 servings.

*If the vegetables are small enough to fall through the grate, you may use a frying pan right on the grill instead.

CORN ON THE COB

4 ears	**corn,** husk on
2 tablespoons	**brown sugar**
I stick	**butter**
	salt and pepper, to taste

Soak corn with husk on in water with brown sugar 30–60 minutes to sweeten and to prevent charring.

Preheat grill to medium-high heat. Remove corn silk at ends of husks by cutting off sharply at end of cob and discard. Place corn on rack and grill, turning frequently, for 20–30 minutes, or until corn is tender. When cool enough to handle, remove husk and any remaining corn silk and serve with butter, salt, and pepper. Makes 4 servings.

VARIATION: Liven up your corn on the cob! Serve it with a light coat of mayonnaise sprinkled with grated Parmesan cheese.

CABBAGE ON THE GRILL

1	**large cabbage head**
	butter
2 teaspoons	**onion powder** or **salt**
	salt and pepper, to taste

Preheat grill to medium heat and lightly oil grate. Cut cabbage into 4–8 wedges, remembering to remove core. Place wedges on a piece of foil big enough to wrap around them completely. Season with butter, onion powder, salt, and pepper. Grill 30 minutes, or until tender. Makes 6–8 servings.

GRILLED SQUASH

2 **acorn squash**
butter
salt and pepper, to taste

Preheat grill to medium heat. Individually wrap each squash in foil with a pat of butter. Grill 30–40 minutes, or until tender. Slice grilled squash in half and scoop out any seeds or strings. Place halves on open foil and add another 2 to 3 pats of butter on top and let cook dry. Serve with butter, salt, and pepper. Makes 4–6 servings.

VARIATION: For a smoky steamed version, grill squash halves over direct heat.

GRILLED ONION BLOOM

I	**large sweet Walla Walla** or **Vidalia onion**
2 tablespoons	**butter**
2 teaspoons	**minced garlic**
	salt and pepper, to taste

Preheat grill to medium heat. Peel onion and slice into fourths or eighths, being careful not cut all the way through and keeping whole onion together. Rub butter and garlic over top. Double wrap onion in aluminum foil, shiny side in, and place on preheated BBQ. Grill 30–40 minutes. Carefully remove from grill and unwrap foil. Season with salt and pepper. Makes 2–4 servings.

GARLIC-CHEDDAR TATERS

6 **russet potatoes**
6 tablespoons **butter**
3 teaspoons **minced garlic**
$^1/_2$ cup **grated cheddar cheese**
salt and pepper, to taste

Preheat grill to medium-high heat. Cut two lengthwise slits two-thirds of the way through each potato, then cut from side to side every $^1/_2$ to 1 inch apart. Carefully hold slits open and divide 1 tablespoon of butter into slits of each potato. Cover each potato with garlic and cheddar cheese. Wrap each potato in aluminum foil, shiny side in, and place on grill. Bake 40–50 minutes, or until potatoes are tender when pierced. Makes 6 servings.

STEVE'S HEAVENLY SAUTEED SWEET ONIONS

2 teaspoons	**minced garlic**
2 tablespoons	**butter**
1 to 2	**large sweet onions,** chopped
$^1/_4$ cup	**grated Parmesan cheese**
	salt and pepper or **seasoning salt,** to taste

Preheat grill to medium-high heat. Place frying pan or flat plate directly on lower rack. Saute garlic in butter 1 minute. Add onions and saute 5–8 minutes, or until tender. Add Parmesan cheese and saute 1 minute more. Season with salt and pepper. Makes 2–4 servings.

VARIATION: This recipe is great over anything grilled!

Breads, Sandwiches, and Pizza

GRILLED GARLIC BREAD

1 loaf	**French** or **Italian bread**
1/2 cup	**mayonnaise**
2 tablespoons	**minced garlic** or **garlic salt**
1/2 cup	**grated Parmesan cheese**

Preheat grill to low heat. Cut bread lengthwise. Place cut side down on grill and lightly toast. Remove bread from grill and set aside. Mix mayonnaise, garlic, and Parmesan cheese. Spread mixture on toasted side of bread. Place back on grill, away from direct flames, cut side up. Grill with lid closed until mixture is hot and melted. Makes 3–5 servings.

HOMEMADE CROUTONS

I loaf	**French bread** (day-old works great)
¹/₂ cup	**olive** or **vegetable oil**
2 tablespoons	**garlic powder**
2 tablespoons	**dried sweet basil**

Preheat grill to medium heat. Cut bread into cubes and place in a bowl. Drizzle bread cubes with oil until lightly covered, then toss with garlic powder and basil. Lightly oil cooking grate of grill and place croutons on grate.* Grill 10–15 minutes, turning frequently until light golden brown and toasted. Makes 6–8 servings.

*To avoid losing bread cubes through the grate, you can use a frying pan directly on the grill.

KELSI'S TUNA MELTS

4 **slices bread**
I can (6 ounces) **tuna,** drained
2–4 tablespoons **mayonnaise,** or according to taste
I tablespoon **sweet pickle relish**
4 **slices cheese**

Preheat grill to medium-high heat. Lightly butter one side of bread slices. Lay bread slices, buttered-side down, on a plate.

In a bowl, combine tuna, mayonnaise, and relish. Top two slices of bread with cheese, and the remaining two slices of bread with tuna mixture. Place bread on grill, buttered side down. Grill 2 minutes, or until cheese melts. Remove from grill and put cheese and tuna halves together to create a sandwich. Makes 2 sandwiches.

VARIATION: Sound too fishy? Try it the Pelham family way—replace the tuna mixture with raspberry jam!

*You can use a frying pan right on top of the grill.

GRILLED AVOCADO BACON SANDWICHES

4 **slices bread**
4 **slices cheese**
6 **slices bacon,** cooked
1 **medium tomato,** sliced
1 **medium avocado,** sliced

Preheat grill to medium-high heat. Lightly butter one side of bread slices. Lay buttered side down on a plate. Top two slices with cheese and place bacon on remaining two slices. Place bread slices on the grill, buttered side down. Grill 2 minutes, or until cheese melts. Remove from grill and add tomato and avocado to the bacon side. Season with salt and pepper. Put the cheese and bacon halves together to create a sandwich. Makes 2 sandwiches.

*You can use a frying pan right on top of the grill.

PIPIN' HOT PIZZA

1	**pizza crust,** ready-made or frozen
1 cup	**tomato sauce**
2^1/$_2$ cups	**grated mozzarella cheese**
^{1}/$_2$ cup	**sliced black olives**
^{1}/$_2$ cup	**sliced mushrooms**
^{1}/$_4$ to ^{1}/$_2$ pound	**sausage,** browned and drained
1 package	**sliced pepperoni**
1	**bell pepper,** sliced
^{1}/$_4$ cup	**chopped sweet onion**

Preheat grill to medium-high heat and lightly oil grate. If using a frozen crust, thaw first, then roll out pizza crust to a size that will fit your grill. Place crust on grill 5 minutes, or until desired doneness. Flip crust over and add sauce, cheese, and other toppings. Cover grill and cook 5–10 minutes, or until cheese is melted and bubbly. Makes 3–5 servings.

GREEK PASTRY PIZZA

1/4 cup	**olive oil**
1/4 teaspoon	**salt**
2 to 4 teaspoons	**minced garlic**
1 loaf	**French, pita, ciabatta,** or **focaccia bread**

Toppings:

2 tablespoons	**fresh basil,** chopped
3	**green onions,** sliced
2	**medium tomatoes,** sliced
1/4 to 1/2 cup	**artichoke hearts**
1 cup	**grated mozzarella cheese**
2 ounces	**crumbled feta cheese**
1/4 cup	**halved olives**

Preheat grill to medium-high heat. Combine oil, salt, and garlic together. Cut bread in half, then cut in half lengthwise. Brush olive oil mixture over cut side of bread. Carefully place sliced bread cut side down on hot grill and toast 1–2 minutes, or until bread begins to brown. Remove from grill. Layer toasted side with toppings. Carefully return to grill (topping side up). Close lid and continue grilling 2–4 minutes, or until bottom has browned and cheese melts. If cheese is slow to melt, move to upper rack of grill and close lid, checking every 1–2 minutes until done. If grill does not have an upper rack, place pizza on aluminum foil in grill to prevent bottom from burning while cheese melts. Makes 3–5 servings.

VARIATION: For a thin crust, scoop out the middle of cut bread and fill the remaining crust with toppings and cheese.

SEAFOOD PESTO PIZZA

2	**loaves focaccia** or **prepared pizza crusts**
4 to 6 ounces	**pesto sauce**
1 1/2 cups	**grated mozzarella cheese**
1/4 cup	**grated Parmesan** or **Romano cheese**
1/2 cup	**ricotta cheese**

Toppings:

1 1/2 cups	**peeled shrimp** (sauteed in butter)
1 cup	**diced crabmeat**
1	**large tomato,** sliced
1/4 cup	**peeled garlic cloves**
1	**large sweet yellow bell pepper,** sliced
5 ounces	**frozen chopped spinach,** thawed and drained
1/2	**sweet onion,** sliced
1 teaspoon	**fresh lemon juice**

Preheat grill to medium-high heat. Place focaccia or pizza crusts on grill and toast 1–2 minutes, or until bread begins to brown. Remove from grill. Top toasted side with pesto sauce and half of all cheeses. Arrange shrimp, crabmeat, tomato, garlic, pepper, spinach, and onion over top. Cover with remaining cheese. Carefully return to grill. Close lid and continue grilling 2–4 minutes, or until bottom browns and cheese melts. If top is slow to melt, move to upper rack and close lid, checking every 1–2 minutes until done. If grill does not have an upper rack, place pizza on aluminum foil in grill to prevent bottom from burning while cheese melts. Sprinkle lemon juice over pizza and serve. Makes 6 servings.

CHEESY QUESADILLAS POR KAY

4 **flour tortillas**
cooking oil or **butter**
2 cups **shredded Monterey Jack** or **cheddar cheese**

Toppings:

grilled sliced chicken
chopped onions
fresh spinach
sliced black olives
diced green chiles

Heat grill to medium-high heat. Brush both sides of tortillas with cooking oil or butter. Place tortillas on grill 1–3 minutes, or until browned. Flip tortillas over and layer half of tortilla with cheese, then add any additional toppings. Grill until cheese melts, then remove from grill and fold plain side of tortillas over toppings. Makes 2–4 servings.

BEEF

SIMPLE STEAK

2 to 4 **steaks** (porterhouse, T-bone, rib eye,
New York, or top sirloin)
Steve's Famous Dry Rub (see Sauces and
Rubs, page 122) or **Montreal Steak Seasoning**
salt and pepper, to taste

Preheat grill to high heat. Sprinkle steaks with dry rub or seasoning.
Sear steaks over direct high heat 1 minute per side. Turn grill down to
medium heat, then cook until desired doneness (see Advanced Grilling
Tips, page 9). Season with salt and pepper. Remove steaks from grill
and allow to sit 2–3 minutes before serving. Makes 2–4 servings.

VARIATION: For more flavor, allow seasoned steaks to sit at room
temperature 20 minutes before grilling.

JAZZED-UP BBQ STEAK

2 to 4 **sirloin steaks**
     Jazzed-Up BBQ Sauce (see Sauces and Rubs, page 122)

Preheat grill to high heat. Sear steaks over direct high heat 1 minute per side then turn grill down to medium heat and cook until desired doneness (see Advanced Grilling Tips, page 9). During last 5 minutes of grilling, coat steaks with sauce, then turn every 1–2 minutes. Remove steaks from grill and allow to sit 2–3 minutes before serving. Makes 2–4 servings.

DOC OLLERTON'S DRY-RUB T-BONE STEAK

2 to 4 **T-bone** or **porterhouse steaks,**
about 1 1/2 inches thick
Steve's Famous Dry Rub (see Sauces
and Rubs, page 122)
smoker pouch (see Helpful Hints, page 7)
8 ounces **fresh sliced mushrooms**
butter

Lightly rub steaks with dry rub then allow them to sit at room temperature 20–30 minutes before grilling. Place smoker pouch directly on the fire under the grate and turn to high heat until smoke begins to rise from holes. Sear steaks over direct high heat 1–2 minutes per side. Turn grill down to medium-low heat. Continue grilling over indirect heat until desired doneness, turning once halfway through grilling time (see Advanced Grilling Tips, page 9).

In a frying pan, combine mushrooms with butter and saute until mushrooms are tender. When steak is done, serve with sauteed mushrooms over top. Makes 2–4 servings.

HONEY GARLIC BBQ BEEF

2 to 4 **sirloin steaks***
Honey Garlic BBQ Sauce (see Sauces and
  Rubs, page 123)
Steve's Heavenly Sauteed Sweet Onions
  (see Vegetables, page 30)

Preheat grill to high heat. Sear steaks over direct high heat 1 minute per
side. Reduce grill to medium heat and cook until desired doneness (see
Advanced Grilling Tips, page 9). During last 5 minutes of cooking, coat
steak with sauce, then turn every 1–2 minutes. Remove steaks from
grill and allow to sit 2–3 minutes.

Prepare Steve's Heavenly Sauteed Sweet Onions when steaks are
nearly done. Serve steaks with a spoonful of onions over top. Makes
2–4 servings.

*4 to 8 boneless beef ribs may be substituted.

COACH'S SAMOAN SIRLOIN STRIPS

1 1/2 pounds   **sirloin tip steak,** cut into 1/2-inch strips
             Coach's Island-Style Marinade (see Sauces and
             Rubs, page 125)

Add steak strips to marinade in a large covered bowl or zipper-lock plastic bag and let marinate overnight. Preheat grill to high heat. Place steak strips on grill 30 seconds per side, then turn grill down to medium heat. Grill 8–12 minutes, or until desired doneness, turning frequently. Makes 2–4 servings.

SMOKY MOP SAUCE STEAKS

         smoker pouch (see Helpful Hints, page 7)
2 to 4 **beef steaks,** any variety
         Mop Sauce (see Sauces and Rubs, page 123)
         BBQ sauce, any variety
         salt and pepper, to taste

Place smoker pouch directly on the fire under the grate and turn to high heat until smoke begins to rise from holes. Turn grill down to medium-low heat. Place steaks on upper rack or use foil under steaks if grill only has one level or cooks hot. Turn steaks every 5–6 minutes, coating with Mop Sauce each time, until desired doneness (see Advanced Grilling Tips, page 9). Season with salt and pepper. Remove steaks from grill and allow to sit 2–3 minutes before serving. Serve with BBQ sauce for dipping. Makes 2–4 servings.

GARLIC STEAKS

2 to 4 **steaks** (porterhouse, T-bone, rib eye, New York,
or top sirloin)
1 tablespoon **minced garlic**
2 tablespoons **rock salt**
Montreal Steak Seasoning, to taste

Rub both sides of steaks with minced garlic and rock salt. Sear steaks
over direct high heat 1 minute per side then, turn grill down to medium
heat and cook until desired doneness (see Advanced Grilling Tips,
page 9). Season with seasoning. Remove from grill and allow to sit
2–3 minutes before serving. Makes 2–4 servings.

TERIYAKI STEAKS

1 cup	**Kikkoman soy sauce**
1 cup	**sugar**
1	**clove fresh garlic,** minced
1 tablespoon	**grated fresh ginger**
3	**green onions,** sliced
2 to 4	**beef steaks,** any variety (cube steak is good here)

Combine all ingredients except steaks in a sauce pan on the stove and heat until sugar dissolves. Pour into a bowl and add steaks. Marinate 1 hour, or no longer than 2 hours, before grilling.

Place steaks over medium-low heat. Grill, turning every 4–5 minutes, until desired doneness (see Advanced Grilling Tips, page 9). Remove steaks from grill and allow to sit 2–3 minutes before serving. Makes 2–4 servings.

PATRICK'S PEPPER STEAK

coarsely crushed peppercorns, to taste
2 to 4 **sirloin steaks**
salt and pepper, to taste

Sprinkle peppercorns on both sides of steaks, pressing into steaks well. Allow them to sit at room temperature 20 minutes before grilling. Sear steaks over direct high heat 1 minute per side, then turn grill down to medium heat and cook until desired doneness (see Advanced Grilling Tips, page 9). Season with salt and pepper. Remove steaks from grill and allow to sit 2–3 minutes before serving. Makes 2–4 servings.

PEPPERED SIRLOIN STEAKS
SMOTHERED IN CREAM SAUCE

Sauce:

$^1/_2$	**sweet onion,** sliced
I teaspoon	**minced garlic**
I tablespoon	**butter**
I teaspoon	**water**
I teaspoon	**white grape juice**
I teaspoon	**apple juice** or **cider**
$^1/_2$ pint	**whipping cream** or **half-and-half**
	salt, to taste

I tablespoon	**coarsely ground black pepper**
2 to 4	**sirloin steaks**

Saute onion and garlic in butter in a large frying pan 5 minutes, or until tender. Add remaining sauce ingredients and bring to a boil, stirring. Season with salt and simmer until ready to serve over steaks.

Press black pepper into steaks and grill to desired doneness (see Advanced Grilling Tips, page 9). Serve with warm cream sauce. Makes 2–4 servings.

STEAKHOUSE SPECIAL

2 to 4 **beef steaks,** any variety
1 cup **nonalcoholic beer**
2 teaspoons **brown sugar**
$1/2$ teaspoon **seasoned salt**
$1/4$ teaspoon **ground black pepper**

Place steaks in a shallow pan and pour beer over top. Marinate 1 hour in the refrigerator. Remove steaks from marinade. Mix together dry ingredients and rub on both sides of steaks. Let sit with dry rub 30 minutes. Preheat grill to high heat. Place steaks on grill 1 minute per side, then turn grill down to medium heat. Grill 10–15 minutes, or until desired doneness, turning frequently. Makes 2–4 servings.

GRANDMA GIBBS' STEAK KABOBS WITH BITE

2 to 4	**country-style beef ribs** or **steaks,** cut into bite-size pieces
1/2 cup	**cider vinegar**
1 cup	**vegetable oil**
1 envelope	**onion soup mix**
2 teaspoons	**gourmet, teriyaki,** or **soy sauce**
2 tablespoons	**minced garlic**

Mix all ingredients together in a bowl. Marinate 2–3 hours. Place steak pieces on skewers.* Grill over medium-high heat until done (see Advanced Grilling Tips, page 9). Makes 2–4 servings.

VARIATION: To make things more interesting, alternate mushrooms, bell pepper wedges, and onion wedges between steak pieces before grilling.

*Soak skewers in water 30 minutes prior to adding meat to prevent burning.

BBQ PRIME RIB ROAST

I	**prime rib roast**
$^1/_2$ cup	**rock salt**
3 tablespoons	**minced garlic**
$^1/_4$ to $^1/_2$ cup	**garlic cloves**

Using wet hands, press a liberal layer of rock salt and minced garlic over roast. Preheat grill to high heat. Sear roast on all sides, 4 minutes per side. Move roast to well-oiled upper rack and place a large dripping pan under roast on lower rack. If the grill only has one level, place meat on double-thick aluminum foil, shiny side up.

Cover roast with whole garlic cloves. Grill 20–30 minutes per pound. Use a meat thermometer to check for doneness, and remove roast from grill when it reaches an internal temperature of 130 degrees (rare) to 150 degrees (medium). Place roast on a platter, cover loosely with foil, and let sit 15 minutes. The meat will continue to cook and the internal temperature should rise around 10 degrees. If you want it cooked more, remove roast from grill at an internal temperature of 165 degrees and let sit 15 minutes before serving. Makes 4–6 servings.

HUNTER'S WEST COAST BBQ RIBS

$^1/_2$ can **cola,** not diet
$^1/_2$ cup **Italian salad dressing**
1 tablespoon **liquid smoke**
3 to 4 pounds **country-style beef ribs**
1 bottle **BBQ sauce,** any variety

Mix cola, Italian dressing, and liquid smoke together in a large bowl. Add meat to the bowl, cover, and marinate overnight. Grill ribs over medium heat, turning frequently, and coating with BBQ sauce during last 5 minutes of total cook time (see Advanced Grilling Tips, page 9). Makes 4–6 servings.

VARIATION: For extra-tender ribs, boil them in water for 1 hour before marinating.

SWEET AND SPICY DRY RUB RIBS

Steve's Famous Dry Rub (see Sauces and
Rubs, page 122)
4 to 8 **country-style beef ribs**
1 ¹/₂ cups **salsa,** divided

Rub dry rub into ribs and let sit about 1 hour before grilling. Preheat
grill to medium heat. Lightly oil the grate. Grill 15–20 minutes, or to
desired doneness, turning frequently. Just before you take ribs off the
grill, brush with ¹/₂ cup of the salsa. Serve ribs with remaining salsa
over top. Makes 3–5 servings.

SMOKED HONEY GARLIC BBQ RIBS

3 to 4 pounds **beef** or **pork ribs**
Honey Garlic BBQ Sauce (see Sauces and Rubs, page 123)
smoker pouch (see Helpful Hints, page 7)

Marinate ribs 30 minutes or overnight in sauce. Place smoker pouch directly on the fire under the grate and turn to high heat until smoke begins to rise from holes. Sear ribs over direct high heat 1 minute per side. Turn grill down to medium heat. Grill 15 to 25 minutes, or to desired doneness, turning frequently. Baste during last 5 minutes of grilling with leftover marinade that has been boiled. Makes 3–5 servings.

ROBERTO'S SOUTH AMERICAN LIME RIBS

4 to 8 **boneless beef ribs**
$^3/_4$ cup **rock salt**
2 tablespoons **minced garlic**
8 **limes,** sectioned

Preheat grill to medium heat. Coat ribs liberally with salt and press in. Sprinkle with garlic. Lightly oil the grill. Grill 15–20 minutes, or to desired doneness, turning frequently. Remove from grill and squeeze limes over top for a great flavor. Makes 3–5 servings.

KOREAN RIBS

1 pound	**beef ribs,** about $1/4$ inch thick
$3/4$ cup	**water**
$3/4$ cup	**soy sauce**
$1/2$ cup	**brown sugar,** firmly packed
$1/2$ cup	**rice** or **cider vinegar**
1 tablespoon	**ketchup**
1 teaspoon	**fresh grated** or **minced ginger**
2 teaspoons	**minced garlic**
2 tablespoons	**sesame oil** (optional)
3 tablespoons	**scallions** or **green onions,** finely chopped

Mix all ingredients together except scallions or green onions. Marinate meat 24 hours or overnight, stirring occasionally. Preheat grill to medium-low heat. Turn grill down to low heat. Grill ribs slowly for about 15–20 minutes, or until done, turning frequently. Garnish with scallions or green onions. Makes 2–4 servings.

VARIATION: For a spicier version, add 1 teaspoon red pepper flakes and/or $1/2$ teaspoon cayenne pepper.

ANDIE'S BBQ BURGERS

I pound	**lean ground beef**
$^1/_2$ envelope	**dry onion soup mix**
$^1/_4$ cup	**ketchup**
2 tablespoons	**brown sugar**
I teaspoon	**vinegar**
I teaspoon	**dry mustard**
	salt and pepper, to taste
4 to 5	**cheese slices**
4 to 5	**hamburger buns**

Preheat grill to medium heat. Thoroughly mix first 7 ingredients together by hand. Then form ground beef mixture into 4 or 5 hamburger patties; remember, they will shrink when cooked. Grill 10–20 minutes, or until done, turning every 4–5 minutes. Add cheese to the burgers, then remove from heat. Serve on hamburger buns. Makes 2–4 servings.

JUICIEST BBQ HAMBURGERS EVER

1 pound	**lean ground beef**
$1/4$ cup	**BBQ sauce**
2 tablespoons	**Worcestershire sauce**
$1/4$	**onion,** finely chopped
$1/4$ cup	**instant oats**
4 to 5	**cheese slices**
4 to 5	**hamburger buns**

Preheat grill to medium heat. Thoroughly mix first 5 ingredients together by hand. Form ground beef mixture into 4 or 5 hamburger patties; remember, they will shrink when cooked. Grill 10–20 minutes, or until done, turning every 4–5 minutes. Add cheese to the burgers and remove from heat. Serve on hamburger buns. Makes 2–4 servings.

STEVE'S DRY RUB BURGERS

I pound **lean ground beef***
Steve's Famous Dry Rub (see Sauces and
Rubs, page 122)
4 to 5 **cheese slices**
4 to 5 **hamburger buns**

Preheat grill to medium heat. Form ground beef into 4 or 5 hamburger
patties; remember they will shrink when cooked. Sprinkle with dry rub
and grill 10–20 minutes, or until done, turning every 4–5 minutes. Add
cheese to the burgers and remove from heat. Serve on hamburger buns.
Makes 2–4 servings.

*For a time-saver, try using pre-made or frozen hamburger patties.

BASIC BRISKET

1	**beef brisket**
	Steve's Famous Dry Rub (see Sauces and Rubs, page 122)
$^1/_2$ cup	**salsa**
$^1/_4$ cup	**chili sauce**
3 tablespoons	**orange marmalade**
	salt and pepper, to taste

Preheat grill to high heat. Seal the juices in brisket by searing it on grill 1–2 minutes per side. Turn grill down to low heat and grill brisket slowly, about 20–30 minutes per pound of meat. Turn frequently until done.

Combine salsa, chili sauce, and orange marmalade, and use as a baste for the brisket during the last 5 minutes of grilling. When brisket is done, season with salt and pepper. Makes 3–5 servings.

SHREDDED BEEF BRISKET

smoker pouch (see Helpful Hints, page 7)
1 (2- to 3-pound) **beef brisket**
Mop Sauce (see Sauces and Rubs, page 123)
2 cups **BBQ sauce,** any variety

Place smoker pouch directly on the fire under the grate and turn to high heat until smoke begins to rise from holes. Immediately turn burner down to medium-low heat. Place brisket on upper rack, or if grill only has one level, use double-thick aluminum foil underneath brisket.

Begin basting with Mop Sauce after 30 minutes of grilling and repeat this process every 30 minutes, until done. Grill until the internal temperature reaches 165–180 degrees, but don't exceed 190 degrees. Remove from grill and allow to sit 10–15 minutes.

Using two forks, shred meat into fine pieces. Mix shredded meat with heated BBQ sauce, or serve it on the side. Serve on a toasted bun with coleslaw on the side or on the sandwich. Makes 4–6 servings.

POULTRY

SIMPLEST BBQ CHICKEN

4 to 6 **boneless, skinless chicken breasts***
thyme or **tarragon**
BBQ sauce, any variety
salt and pepper, to taste

Grill chicken 20–30 minutes over medium-low heat, turning frequently, until done. To check for doneness, squeeze chicken to see if juices run clear. If you aren't satisfied, cut open to check. Sprinkle a light coating of thyme or tarragon over chicken. Baste with BBQ sauce during the last 5 minutes of grilling, turning every 1–2 minutes. Season with salt and pepper. Serve chicken as desired. Great on Caesar salads. Makes 4–6 servings.

*A whole chicken, cut and quartered, can also be used. Grill 30–40 minutes.

MELISSA'S JAZZED-UP BBQ CHICKEN

4 to 6 **boneless, skinless chicken breasts***
Jazzed-Up BBQ Sauce (see Sauces and Rubs, page 122)
2 **red bell peppers,** sliced
1 **yellow onion,** sliced
1 tablespoon **butter**

Preheat grill to medium-low heat. Grill chicken 20–30 minutes, turning frequently, until done. To check for doneness, squeeze chicken to see if juices run clear. If you aren't satisfied, cut open to check. Baste chicken with sauce during last 5 minutes of cooking, turning every 1–2 minutes. Remove chicken from grill and allow to sit 2–3 minutes before serving.

Combine red peppers, onion, and butter in a frying pan and saute until tender. Serve over chicken. Makes 4–6 servings.

*A whole chicken, cut and quartered, can also be used. Grill 30–40 minutes.

SCOTT'S TANTALIZING DRY RUB CHICKEN—ON A CAN

	smoker pouch (see Helpful Hints, page 7)
I tablespoon	**coarse salt**
I tablespoon	**sugar**
I tablespoon	**celery salt**
I tablespoon	**brown sugar**
I tablespoon	**garlic salt**
I tablespoon	**ground black pepper**
2 tablespoons	**paprika**
2 tablespoons	**butter** (optional)
I	**whole chicken**
I can (12 ounces)	**non-diet soda** (Dr. Pepper works good here)

Place smoker pouch directly on the fire under the grate and turn to high heat until smoke begins to rise from holes. Immediately turn down to medium-low heat. Combine all dry ingredients together in a bowl. Rub butter, if desired, over chicken. Then rub dry ingredients into chicken thoroughly. Let sit at least 30 minutes.

Remove the upper grill rack and see if the whole chicken fits standing up in the grill with the lid down. If the chicken fits, remove chicken and set the can of soda, opened, on the grill. Stand the chicken over top of the can, so the can is in its inner cavity. If grill cooks hot, use double-thick aluminum foil underneath chicken. Grill 20 minutes per pound, or until done.

If the chicken doesn't fit standing, cut it up and grill it without the soda. Turn chicken every 5–10 minutes, until done. To check doneness, squeeze chicken to see if juices run clear. If you aren't satisfied, cut open to check. Makes 3–5 servings.

SMOKED HONEY GARLIC BBQ CHICKEN

4 to 6 **boneless, skinless chicken breasts***
Honey Garlic BBQ Sauce (see Sauces and
Rubs, page 123)
smoker pouch (see Helpful Hints, page 7)
cinnamon

Marinate chicken in sauce at least 30 minutes, or overnight. Place smoker pouch directly on the fire under the grate and turn to high heat until smoke begins to rise from holes. Turn grill down to low heat. Grill chicken 20–30 minutes, or until done, turning frequently. To check doneness, squeeze chicken to see if juices run clear. If you aren't satisfied, cut open to check. Lightly sprinkle cinnamon over chicken before serving. Makes 4–6 servings.

*A whole chicken, cut and quartered, can also be used. Grill 30–40 minutes.

SMOKY MOPPED CHICKEN

smoker pouch (see Helpful Hints, page 7)
4 to 6 **boneless, skinless chicken breasts***
Mop Sauce (see Sauces and Rubs, page 123)
BBQ sauce, any variety

Place smoker pouch directly on the fire under the grate and turn to high heat until smoke begins to rise from holes. Immediately turn grill down to low heat. Place chicken on upper grill rack, or on aluminum foil if grill only has one level or cooks hot. Turn chicken every 4–5 minutes, coating with Mop Sauce each time, until done. To check doneness, squeeze chicken to see if juices run clear. If you aren't satisfied, cut open to check. Serve with BBQ sauce. Makes 4–6 servings.

*A whole chicken, cut and quartered, can also be used. Grill 30–40 minutes.

MORRIS'S ALABAMA-STYLE BBQ CHICKEN

4 to 6 **boneless, skinless chicken breasts***
Alabama White BBQ Sauce (see Sauces and
Rubs, page 124)

Preheat grill to low heat. Grill chicken, turning every 4–5 minutes, until done. To check doneness, squeeze chicken to see if juices run clear. If you aren't satisfied, cut open to check. Prior to basting, set some BBQ sauce aside for dipping. During last 5 minutes of cooking, coat chicken with BBQ sauce, turning every 1–2 minutes. Serve hot with extra sauce for dipping. Makes 4–6 servings.

*A whole chicken, cut and quartered, can also be used. Grill 30–40 minutes.

GRANDMA'S BBQ COLA CHICKEN

I cup **flour**
1 1/2 pounds **chicken tenders***
I bottle **ketchup**
1/2 can **cola,** not diet

Preheat grill to low heat. Place flour in a bowl and roll chicken in it.

In a separate bowl, mix ketchup and cola thoroughly, then set aside. Grill chicken 20–30 minutes, or until done, turning every 4–5 minutes. During last 5 minutes, coat chicken with cola sauce. To check doneness, squeeze chicken to see if juices run clear. If you aren't satisfied, cut open to check. Makes 3–5 servings.

*A whole chicken, cut and quartered, can also be used. Grill 30–40 minutes.

JANICE'S TANGY CHICKEN

4 to 6 **boneless, skinless chicken breasts***
1 cup **cider vinegar**
$^1/_2$ cup **vegetable oil**
3 teaspoons **minced garlic**
$^1/_2$ teaspoon **poultry seasoning**
1 tablespoon **coarse salt**

Mix all ingredients together in a bowl, cover and marinate overnight. Preheat grill to low heat. Grill chicken 20–30 minutes, or until done, turning every 4–5 minutes. To check doneness, squeeze chicken to see if juices run clear. If you aren't satisfied, cut open to check. Makes 4–6 servings.

*A whole chicken, cut and quartered, can also be used. Grill 30–40 minutes.

TAPASA'S SAMOAN-STYLE CHICKEN

8 to 10 **boneless, skinless chicken thighs**
Coach's Island-Style Marinade (see Sauces and
Rubs, page 125)

Marinate chicken in sauce in a covered large bowl or zipper-lock plastic bag overnight. Preheat grill to low heat. Grill chicken, turning every 4–5 minutes, until done. To check doneness, squeeze chicken to see if juices run clear. If you aren't satisfied, cut open to check. Makes 3–5 servings.

ISLAND GRILLED TERIYAKI CHICKEN

8 to 10	**boneless, skinless chicken thighs**
2 cups	**Yoshida's Gourmet Sauce** or **teriyaki sauce**
1 tablespoon	**minced garlic,** to taste
$1/2$	**medium sweet onion,** finely chopped
2	**green onions** or **scallions,** chopped

Mix all ingredients together and marinate in a large covered bowl or zipper-lock plastic bag overnight. Preheat grill to low heat. Grill chicken, turning every 4–5 minutes, until done. To check doneness, squeeze chicken to see if juices run clear. If you aren't satisfied, cut open to check. Makes 3–5 servings.

TAP'S SUCCULENT CHICKEN

3/4 cup **soy sauce**
1 1/2 cups **water**
3/4 cup **brown sugar**
1 1/2 teaspoons **minced garlic**
3 teaspoons **lemon juice**
1 teaspoon **finely minced ginger**
3 to 4 **chopped green onions**
8 to 10 **boneless, skinless chicken thighs**

Mix all ingredients together and marinate in a large covered bowl or zipper-lock plastic bag overnight. Preheat grill to low heat. Grill chicken, turning every 4–5 minutes, until done. To check doneness, squeeze chicken to see if juices run clear. If you aren't satisfied, cut open to check. Makes 3–5 servings.

JEN'S EGYPTIAN GRILLED CHICKEN

4	**boneless, skinless chicken breasts**
1 cup	**plain yogurt**
3 tablespoons	**fresh lemon juice**
3 teaspoons	**minced garlic**
1 teaspoon	**salt**
$1/2$ teaspoon	**ground cinnamon**
$1/2$ teaspoon	**pepper**
$1/4$ teaspoon	**ground cloves**
$1/4$ teaspoon	**ground cardamom***

Mix all ingredients together and marinate in a large covered bowl or zipper-lock plastic bag overnight. Preheat grill to low heat. Grill chicken, turning every 4–5 minutes, until done. To check doneness, squeeze chicken to see if juices run clear. If you aren't satisfied, cut open to check. Makes 4 servings.

*This expensive spice adds a lot of flavor, but it can be left out. Try finding a grocer that sells spices by the bulk and only purchase what you need. This will save you money.

STUFFED CHICKEN BREAST

¹/₂ **sweet onion,** sliced
I tablespoon **minced garlic**
2 tablespoons **butter**
8 (6–8 ounce) **boneless, skinless chicken breasts**
flour
salt and pepper, to taste

Preheat grill to medium-low heat. Saute onion and garlic in butter. Cut a pocket in the side of each chicken breast and stuff with onion mixture. Roll each breast in flour. Grill chicken, turning every 4–5 minutes, until done. To check doneness, squeeze chicken to see if juices run clear. If you aren't satisfied, cut open to check. Season with salt and pepper. Makes 6–8 servings.

BACON-STUFFED CHICKEN BREAST

8 (6–8 ounce) **boneless, skinless chicken breasts**
8 **slices bacon,** cooked
flour
salt and pepper, to taste

Preheat grill to medium-low heat. Cut a pocket in the side of each chicken breast and stuff with a slice of cooked bacon. Roll each breast in flour and then place on grill. Turn chicken every 4–5 minutes until done. Season with salt and pepper. Makes 8 servings.

CRABBY STUFFED CHICKEN BREAST

Stuffing:

I can (6 ounces)	**crabmeat**
I package (8 ounces)	**cream cheese,** softened
I tablespoon	**minced garlic**
$^1/_4$ cup	**grated Parmesan cheese**

8 (6–8 ounce)	**boneless, skinless chicken breasts**
	flour
	salt and pepper, to taste

Preheat grill to medium-low heat. Combine stuffing ingredients. Cut a pocket in the side of each chicken breast and fill with a heaping tablespoon of stuffing. Roll each breast in flour. Grill chicken, turning every 4–5 minutes, until done. To check doneness, squeeze chicken to see if juices run clear. Season with salt and pepper. Makes 8 servings.

ORANGE SESAME CHICKEN

¹/₂ cup	**orange juice**
1 tablespoon	**lemon juice**
1 tablespoon	**vinegar**
2 teaspoons	**mustard**
2 tablespoons	**toasted sesame oil**
8	**boneless, skinless chicken thighs**
	salt and pepper, to taste

Mix the orange juice, lemon juice, vinegar, and mustard in a bowl.
Whisk sesame oil in slowly. Put chicken in a shallow baking dish or a
zipper-lock plastic bag, pour half of marinade over chicken, and chill 2
hours. Grill chicken over medium-low heat, turning every 4–5 minutes,
until done. During last 5 minutes of grilling, coat with reserved marinade.
To check for doneness, squeeze chicken to see if juices run clear. If you
aren't satisfied, cut open to check. Sprinkle toasted sesame seeds over
cooked chicken as a garnish. Makes 8 servings.

GRILLED CHILI SAUCE CHICKEN

1 1/2 cups	**chili sauce**
3/4 cup	**red-wine vinegar**
1 tablespoon	**horseradish**
2 tablespoons	**minced garlic**
1/2 teaspoon	**salt**
4	**boneless, skinless chicken breasts**

Mix all ingredients together except chicken in a large bowl. Reserve half of marinade. Add chicken to bowl and marinate 30 minutes. Preheat grill to medium-low heat. Grill chicken, turning every 4–5 minutes, until done. During last 5 minutes of grilling, coat with reserved marinade. To check doneness, squeeze chicken to see if juices run clear. If you aren't satisfied, cut open to check.

Heat any remaining marinade in a small saucepan until it comes to a full boil, stirring occasionally. Serve with chicken. Makes 4 servings.

ITALIAN CHICKEN

I bottle	**Italian salad dressing**
$^1/_2$ teaspoon	**salt**
$^1/_4$ teaspoon	**pepper**
$^1/_2$ cup	**salsa**
I teaspoon	**Worcestershire sauce**
$^1/_4$ to $^1/_2$ cup	**diced sweet onion**
I teaspoon	**minced garlic**
$^1/_2$ to I cup	**orange juice**
I $^1/_2$ pounds	**boneless, skinless chicken tenders,**

With a wire whisk, mix all ingredients together except chicken in a bowl. Reserve half of marinade. Add chicken to bowl and marinate, covered, at least 30 minutes or overnight. Preheat grill to medium-low heat. Grill chicken, turning every 4–5 minutes, until done. During last 5 minutes of grilling, coat with reserved marinade. To check doneness, squeeze chicken to see if juices run clear. If you aren't satisfied, cut open to check. Makes 3–5 servings.

GRANT'S MONDAY-NIGHT SPECIAL BUFFALO WINGS

1 cup	**spicy BBQ sauce**
2 to 3 tablespoons	**Tabasco sauce,** or according to taste
2 tablespoons	**brown sugar**
1 tablespoon	**vinegar**
$1/4$ teaspoon	**freshly ground black pepper**
2 dozen	**chicken wings**

In a small saucepan, combine all ingredients except wings and bring to a boil. Remove from heat, pour into a large bowl, and let cool 15 minutes. Add chicken wings to marinade and chill 2 hours or more. Grill wings 10–15 minutes over medium-low heat, or until done, turning every 4–5 minutes. To check doneness, squeeze chicken to see if juices run clear. If you aren't satisfied, cut open to check. Serve with celery and a creamy blue cheese salad dressing for dipping. Makes 2–4 servings.

JAZZY BBQ TURKEY LEGS

 2 to 4 **turkey legs**
 Jazzed-Up BBQ Sauce (see Sauces and
 Rubs, page 122)

Preheat grill to medium-high heat. Grill turkey 30–45 minutes, turning occasionally, until done. During the last 5 minutes of cooking, coat turkey with BBQ sauce. Serve hot with any extra sauce, heated, on the side. Makes 2–4 servings.

SMOKED HONEY GARLIC BBQ TURKEY

2 to 4 **turkey breasts**
Honey Garlic BBQ Sauce (see Sauces and Rubs, page 123)
smoker pouch (see Helpful Hints, page 7)
2 **green bell peppers,** sliced
olive oil

Add turkey to sauce and marinate at least 30 minutes or overnight. Place smoker pouch directly on the fire under the grate and turn to high heat until smoke begins to rise from holes. Immediately turn down to medium-low heat. Place turkey on upper rack for best smoking. Cook turkey 20–30 minutes, turning frequently, until done. To check doneness, squeeze to see if juices run clear. If you aren't satisfied, cut open to check.

In a frying pan, saute peppers in butter until tender and serve over turkey. Makes 2–4 servings.

PORK

ROCKIN' CHOPS

2 to 4 **center-cut pork chops** or **steaks,** 1 inch thick
Brine (see Sauces and Rubs, page 124)
salt and pepper, to taste

Marinate pork chops in Brine 2 hours. Preheat grill to medium heat.
Grill chops 6 minutes per side. Move chops to upper rack and turn grill
down to medium-low heat. If there is no upper rack, place chops on
double-thick aluminum foil, shiny side up, on grill. Cook 10 minutes
more, or until done. The internal temperature should be 160 degrees.
Season with salt and pepper. Makes 2–4 servings.

VARIATION: Use BBQ sauce or Steve's Famous Dry Rub (see Sauces and
Rubs, page 122) to add a different flavor.

JAZZED-UP BBQ PORK STEAKS

2 to 4 **center-cut pork chops** or **steaks,** 1 inch thick
Jazzed-Up BBQ Sauce, divided (see Sauces and
Rubs, page 122)
cayenne

Marinate pork in half of sauce at least 30 minutes before grilling. Set
remaining sauce aside. Preheat grill to medium heat. Grill 15–20 minutes,
or to desired doneness. Internal temperature should be 160 degrees.

Add a pinch of cayenne to reserved sauce. During last 5 minutes of cook-
ing, coat chops or steaks with reserved sauce; turn every 1–2 minutes.
Remove pork from grill and allow to sit 2–3 minutes before serving.
Makes 2–4 servings.

DRY RUB PORK CHOPS

2 to 4 **center-cut pork chops** or **steaks,** 1 inch thick
Big Red's Spicy Dry Rub (see Sauces and
Rubs, page 123)
1 cup **BBQ sauce,** any variety

Rub pork thoroughly with dry rub and marinate 20–40 minutes before grilling. Preheat grill to medium heat. Place pork on grill over medium-low heat, 6 minutes per side, then move to upper rack and turn down to low heat. If there is no upper rack, place ribs on double-thick aluminum foil, shiny side up, on grill. Cook 10 more minutes, or until done. The internal temperature should be 160 degrees. Serve with BBQ sauce. Makes 2–4 servings.

VARIATION: Try Steve's Famous Dry Rub (see Sauces and Rubs, page 122) in place of Big Red's Spicy Dry Rub.

PERFECT RUBBED RIBS

I to 2 **racks pork ribs** or **pork spareribs***
Steve's Famous Dry Rub (see Sauces and
Rubs, page 122)

Peel film off back of ribs by hand, or carefully with a knife. Rub the ribs
thoroughly with dry rub about I hour before grilling. Preheat grill to
medium-low heat. Cook ribs slowly 30–40 minutes, or until done.
Makes 2–4 servings.

VARIATION: To help your ribs have a more robust flavor, soak them in
Brine (see Sauces and Rubs, page 124) I–2 hours before grilling.

*Ask your grocer's meat department to rip (or cut) ribs lengthwise to
create bite-size riblets.

DRY RUB PULLED PORK

smoker pouch (see Helpful Hints, page 7)
1 (3–5 pound) **pork shoulder roast**
Steve's Famous Dry Rub (see Sauces and Rubs, page 122)
2 cups **BBQ sauce,** any variety

Place smoker pouch directly on the fire under the grate and turn to high heat until smoke begins to rise from holes. Immediately turn down to medium-low heat. Rub roast thoroughly with dry rub and cook on upper grill rack, or use aluminum foil underneath it if grill only has one level. Grill 15–20 minutes per pound, or until the internal temperature reaches 165–180 degrees. Turn roast every 15–20 minutes, until done. Remove from grill and allow to sit 10–15 minutes. Using two forks, tear meat into fine shreds. Mix shredded meat with heated BBQ sauce, or serve separately. Serve on a toasted bun or bread with coleslaw on the side or on the sandwich. Makes 3–5 servings.

VARIATION: For a spicier version, use Big Red's Spicy Dry Rub (see Sauces and Rubs, page 123) instead.

SMOKED HONEY GARLIC BBQ PORK

Honey Garlic BBQ Sauce (see Sauces and
  Rubs, page 123)
$^1/_4$ teaspoon **curry**
2 to 4 **center-cut pork chops** or **steaks,** 1 inch thick
  smoker pouch (see Helpful Hints, page 7)

Combine Honey Garlic BBQ Sauce with curry. Marinate pork in sauce
30–60 minutes before grilling. Place smoker pouch directly on the fire
under the grate and turn to high heat until smoke begins to rise from
holes. Immediately turn down to medium-low heat. Grill pork 15–20
minutes on the upper rack for best smoking results. The internal
temperature should reach 160 degrees. During last 5 minutes of cooking, coat pork with sauce, turning every 2 minutes. Remove from grill
and allow to sit 2–3 minutes before serving. Makes 2–4 servings.

SMOKED & MOPPED PULLED PORK

	smoker pouch (see Helpful Hints, page 7)
1 (3–5 pound)	**pork shoulder roast**
	Mop Sauce (see Sauces and Rubs, page 123)
2 cups	**BBQ sauce,** any variety

Place smoker pouch directly on the fire under the grate and turn to high heat until smoke begins to rise from holes. Immediately turn down to medium heat. Place roast on upper grill rack, or use foil under roast if grill only has one level. Begin basting roast after 30 minutes of grilling, and repeat this process every 30 minutes, until done. Grill until the internal temperature reaches 165–180 degrees, turning every 15–20 minutes. Remove from grill and allow to sit 10–15 minutes.

Using two forks, tear meat into fine shreds. Mix shredded meat with heated BBQ sauce, or serve separately. Serve on a toasted bun or bread with coleslaw on the side or on the sandwich. Makes 4–6 servings.

FLOYD'S DOCTORED-UP PORK STEAKS

2 to 4 **center-cut pork chops** or **steaks,** 1 inch thick
Brine (see Sauces and Rubs, page 124)
Floyd's Fantastic Sauce (see Sauces and
Rubs, page 125)

Marinate pork in Brine and chill 30–60 minutes. Grill chops 6–10 minutes per side over medium-low heat. Move to upper grate and turn down to low heat. If there is no upper rack, place ribs on double-thick aluminum foil, shiny side up, on grill. Cook 10 minutes more, or until done. The internal temperature should be 160 degrees. During last 5 minutes of grilling, coat pork with Floyd's Fantastic Sauce. Makes 2–4 servings.

CILANTRO PORK STEAK

2 **pork steaks** or **pork chops**
1 cup **chopped fresh cilantro leaves**
salt and pepper, to taste
garlic salt, to taste

Preheat grill to medium-low heat. Sprinkle pork with some of the cilantro leaves and grill 20 minutes, turning every 4–5 minutes, coating with cilantro leaves each time. Season with salt, pepper, and garlic salt. Makes 2 servings.

CHRIS'S KICKIN' MUSTARD RIBS

1 cup	**mustard**
1/4 cup	**honey**
2 tablespoons	**paprika**
1/4 cup	**brown sugar**
1 tablespoon	**garlic powder**
1 1/2 to 2 tablespoons	**cider vinegar**
1 to 2 tablespoons	**chili powder**
1 to 2	**racks pork ribs** or **pork spareribs***

Preheat grill to medium-low heat. Mix all ingredients together except ribs. Peel film off back of ribs by hand, or carefully with a knife. Spread the sauce over ribs. Cook slowly 30–45 minutes, or until done. Makes 2–4 servings.

VARIATION: To help your ribs have a more robust flavor soak them in Brine (see Sauces and Rubs page) for 1-2 hours prior to grilling.

*Ask your butcher to cut the ribs lengthwise to create bite-size riblets.

GRILLED PORK CITRUS STEAKS

3 tablespoons **butter**
1 teaspoon **minced garlic**
1 teaspoon **lemon juice**
$^1/_4$ cup **heavy whipping cream** or **half-and-half**
4 to 5 **pork chops**

Melt butter in a small saucepan over medium heat. Stir in garlic and add lemon juice. Heat until garlic is tender. Add cream and heat through. Remove from heat and set aside.

Preheat grill to medium-high heat and lightly oil grate then turn grill down to medium heat. Place chops on grill, sear 1 minute per side, then coat sides with cream mixture. Cover and grill 3–5 minutes more per side, brushing both sides again with cream mixture during the last 2 minutes. Grill until done or when internal temperature reaches 160 degrees. Makes 3–5 servings.

VARIATION: For more moist pork, marinate in Brine (see Sauces and Rubs, page 124) 30–60 minutes before grilling.

SPICY RUBBED PORK ROAST

smoker pouch (see Helpful Hints, page 7)
1 (3–5 pound) **pork shoulder roast**
Big Red's Spicy Dry Rub (see Sauces and Rubs, page 123)
2 cups **BBQ sauce,** any variety

Place smoker pouch directly on the fire under the grate and turn to high heat until smoke begins to rise from holes. Immediately turn down to medium-low heat. Rub roast thoroughly with dry rub, then place on upper grill rack, or use aluminum foil underneath the roast if grill only has one level. Grill 15–20 minutes per pound, or until the internal temperature reaches 165–180 degrees. Turn roast once every 15–20 minutes, until done. Remove from grill and allow to sit 10–15 minutes.

Using two forks, tear meat into fine shreds. Mix shredded meat with heated BBQ sauce. Serve on a toasted bun or bread with coleslaw on the side or on the sandwich. Makes 4–6 servings.

ORANGE SALSA RIBS

I rack **pork ribs** or **pork spare ribs***
Brine (see Sauces and Rubs page 124)
Steve's Famous Dry Rub (see Sauces and
Rubs page 122)

Sauce:
$^1/_2$ cup **salsa**
$^1/_4$ cup **chili sauce**
3 tablespoons **orange marmalade**

Peel film off of the back of the ribs by hand or carefully with a knife.
Rub Dry Rub thoroughly into ribs 60 minutes or less before grilling.

In a bowl, combine all sauce ingredients together. Cook ribs slowly,
30–40 minutes on medium-low heat, or until done. Baste with sauce
during last 5 minutes of grilling.

VARIATION: To help your ribs have a more robust flavor soak them in
Brine (see Sauces and Rubs page) for 1-2 hours prior to grilling.

*Ask your grocer's meat department to rip (or cut) ribs lengthwise to
create bite-size riblets.

SEAFOOD

SHARON'S SUPER SALMON

1 (2–3 pound)	**salmon fillet**
1/2 cup	**mayonnaise**
2 teaspoons	**lemon juice**
	dried onions
	dill
	salt and pepper, to taste

Arrange salmon fillet on the shiny side of double-thick aluminum foil big enough to wrap fillet in. Mix mayonnaise and lemon juice, then spread over salmon. Sprinkle desired amount of dried onions and dill over top. Seal foil wrap around salmon. Grill 20–25 minutes over medium heat, or until fish flakes and is no longer translucent. Season with salt and pepper. Makes 3–5 servings.

MY BIG BRO'S SALMON FOIL SPECIALTY

1 (2–3 pound)	**salmon fillet**
1	**large sweet onion,** sliced
1/4 to 1/2 cup	**scallops,** chopped
2	**medium yellow squash,** chopped
1	**medium zucchini,** chopped
1 pound	**small red** or **new potatoes,** chopped
1/2 cup	**mayonnaise**
2 teaspoons	**lemon juice**
	salt and pepper, to taste

Arrange salmon fillet on double-thick aluminum foil, big enough to wrap fillet and vegetables in. Place onion, scallops, squash, zucchini, and potatoes around salmon. Mix mayonnaise and lemon juice and spread over top of salmon. Place a few onion slices over top mayonnaise mixture. Seal foil wrap around salmon and vegetables. Grill 20–25 minutes over medium heat, or until fish flakes and is no longer translucent. Season with salt and pepper. Makes 3–5 servings.

J.W.'S CEDAR PLANK SALMON WITH BROWN SUGAR RUB

I (2–3 pound)	**salmon fillet**
	cedar plank
I cup	**brown sugar**
I teaspoon	**salt** or **seasoning salt**
1/2 teaspoon	**freshly ground black pepper**
1/4 cup	**olive oil**

Soak a cedar plank (try a piece of untreated fence board) in cold water at least 15 minutes. Preheat grill to medium heat. Mix together brown sugar, salt, and pepper. Coat salmon with olive oil, then liberally rub mixed dry ingredients into salmon. Place salmon on cedar plank, then put cedar plank directly on grill. Grill 20–30 minutes, or until fish flakes and is no longer translucent. Makes 3–5 servings.

BACON-WRAPPED SHRIMP

24 **large shrimp,** peeled and deveined
12 **slices bacon**

Preheat grill to medium heat. Wrap shrimp with half slice of bacon and secure with a toothpick, or put the bacon-wrapped shrimp on a skewer. Lightly oil grate and place shrimp on grill. Grill 3–4 minutes, turning frequently. When bacon is fully cooked, serve. Makes 4–6 servings.

BASIL SHRIMP

2 1/2 tablespoons	**olive oil**
1/2 cup	**butter,** melted and divided
1 1/2	**lemons,** juiced
3 tablespoons	**mustard**
2 tablespoons	**minced fresh basil**
3 cloves	**garlic,** minced (reserve some for dipping sauce)
2 to 3 pounds	**fresh large shrimp,** peeled and deveined
	salt and pepper, to taste

Mix together olive oil and 1/4 cup melted butter. Then stir in lemon juice, mustard, basil, and garlic. Add shrimp, then toss to coat. Cover and chill 1 hour. Preheat grill to medium heat. Remove shrimp from marinade and slide onto skewers.

Lightly oil grate, and arrange skewers on grill. Grill 3–4 minutes, turning every 1–2 minutes, or until done. Combine remaining melted butter and minced garlic for dipping. Season with salt and pepper. Makes 4–6 servings.

SIMPLE WHITE FISH

4 **halibut** or **pike fillets**
4 tablespoons **butter**
3 to 4 teaspoons **fresh marjoram**

Preheat grill to medium heat. Place individual fish fillets on a piece of aluminum foil. Dot each with 1 tablespoon butter and sprinkle with $^1/_2$ to 1 teaspoon marjoram. Fold foil tightly over fish. Place on grill 15–20 minutes over medium heat, or until done. Makes 4 servings.

GRILLED PARMESAN HALIBUT

1	**medium sweet onion,** sliced
2 tablespoons	**minced garlic**
$1/4$ cup	**butter,** melted
2 teaspoons	**Dijon mustard**
2 tablespoons	**lemon juice**
$1/4$ cup	**grated Parmesan cheese**
2 to 4	**halibut steaks,** about $1/3$ pound each
	salt and pepper, to taste

In a frying pan, saute onion and garlic in butter until tender. Then add mustard, lemon juice, and Parmesan cheese. Simmer 3 minutes. Cover halibut with mixture before and during grilling. Grill 15–20 minutes over medium heat, turning once. Pour any remaining marinade over steaks. Season with salt and pepper. Makes 2–4 servings.

LEMON CILANTRO FISH STEAKS

1 1/2 pounds	**salmon, swordfish,** or **halibut steaks,** about 3/4 to 1 inch thick
1 teaspoon	**salt**
1/4 teaspoon	**pepper**
1/4 cup	**butter,** melted
1 tablespoon	**lemon juice**
1 teaspoon	**chopped fresh cilantro leaves**
	lemon wedges

Sprinkle fish with salt and pepper. Mix butter, lemon juice, and cilantro. Cover fish with foil and grill 15–25 minutes over medium heat, brushing 2–3 times with butter mixture. Fish is done when it flakes easily with a fork. Serve with lemon wedges. Makes 2–4 servings.

CRAB-STUFFED MUSHROOMS

$^3/_4$ pound	**medium fresh whole mushrooms**
I can (7.5 ounces)	**crabmeat**
4 tablespoons	**breadcrumbs,** divided
2	**eggs,** lightly beaten
2 tablespoons	**mayonnaise**
2 tablespoons	**finely chopped sweet onion**
I teaspoon	**lemon juice**
$^1/_8$ teaspoon	**ground black pepper**
4 tablespoons	**butter,** melted and divided

Preheat grill to medium heat. Remove stems from mushrooms, then brush caps with some melted butter. Drain and flake crabmeat, then combine with 2 tablespoons breadcrumbs, eggs, mayonnaise, onion, lemon juice, pepper, and 2 tablespoons butter in small bowl. Fill each mushroom cap with some of the crab mixture. Combine remaining breadcrumbs and 2 tablespoons melted butter, then sprinkle over crab stuffing. Grill 5–15 minutes over medium heat. Makes 2–4 servings.

CREAMY CRAB-STUFFED MUSHROOMS

3/4 pound **fresh mushrooms**
1 package (8 ounces) **cream cheese,** softened
1/2 cup **finely crushed croutons**
1/4 cup **Parmesan cheese**
1/8 teaspoon **minced fresh garlic**
1/2 pound **crabmeat**
paprika, to taste

Clean mushrooms and remove stems. Mix cream cheese with crushed croutons, Parmesan cheese, and garlic until fluffy. Shred crabmeat and stir into cream cheese mixture. Place a spoonful of mixture into each mushroom cap, then dust with paprika. Grill 5–15 minutes over medium heat. Makes 2–4 servings.

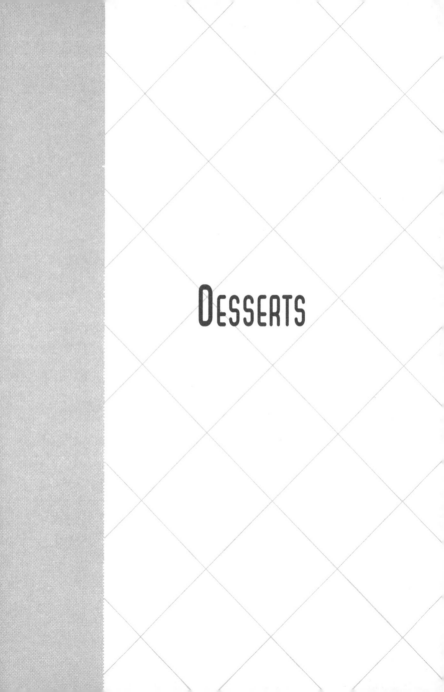

DESSERTS

GRILLED APPLE DELIGHT

$^1/_4$ cup **sugar**
1 tablespoon **cinnamon**
nutmeg, to taste
1 tablespoon **oatmeal**
$^1/_4$ cup **brown sugar**
4 **medium red** or **golden delicious apples,**
cut into $^1/_4$-inch-thick slices

Preheat grill to medium-high heat. Mix sugar, cinnamon, nutmeg, oatmeal, and brown sugar in a bowl. Roll apple slices in mixture. Grill 3–4 minutes, turning every minute, or until tender. Makes 3–5 servings.

PERFECT PEARS

$^1/_4$ cup **sugar**
1 tablespoon **cinnamon**
4 **medium pears,** cut into $^1/_4$-inch-thick slices

Preheat grill to medium-high heat. Mix sugar and cinnamon in a bowl. Cover pear slices with sugar mixture. Grill 5–8 minutes, turning every minute, or until tender. Makes 3–5 servings.

RYAN'S TASTY BANANA TREATS

2	**ripe bananas,** unpeeled
$1/4$ cup	**brown sugar**
2 teaspoons	**cinnamon**

Preheat grill to medium-high heat. Place unpeeled bananas on grill 4–6 minutes, turning frequently until peel is blackened. Remove from grill, then peel and slice bananas into bite-size pieces. Roll in sugar and cinnamon mixture and serve. Makes 2 servings.

JUST PEACHIE

2	**large peaches**
2 tablespoons	**orange juice**
	brown sugar
	vanilla ice cream or **frozen yogurt**

Clean, halve, and pit peaches, then brush with orange juice. Roll peaches in brown sugar, then place them cut side up on grill. Spoon any excess orange juice into centers followed by more brown sugar. Grill 3–5 minutes, or until sugar is lightly caramelized. Transfer to serving dishes and top with scoop of ice cream or frozen yogurt. Makes 4 servings.

CHOCOLATE BANANA BANG-A-RANG

2 **ripe bananas,** unpeeled
4 scoops **vanilla ice cream**
4 tablespoons **hot fudge sauce**

Preheat grill to medium-high heat. Place unpeeled bananas on grill 4–6 minutes, turning frequently until peel is blackened. Remove from grill, then peel and slice bananas lengthwise. Serve topped with vanilla ice cream and hot fudge. Makes 2 servings.

BANANA DREAM BOAT

4 **ripe bananas,** unpeeled
$^1/_2$ cup **small marshmallows**
$^1/_2$ cup **chocolate chips**

Preheat grill to medium-high heat. Clean unpeeled bananas, then slice a wedge lengthwise in center of bananas, removing the long section from tip to tip. Fill the space with a mixture of marshmallows and chocolate chips. Place on grill with open side up. Grill until chocolate and marshmallows melt. Remove and serve hot with a spoon. Makes 4 servings.

COULD IT BE CANTALOUPE

1 **cantaloupe**
$^1/_2$ cup **sugar**

Preheat grill to medium heat. Cut cantaloupe into chunks and put on skewers. Dust cantaloupe with a liberal amount of sugar and place on lightly oiled grill. Cook 4–7 minutes, turning frequently. Makes 4–6 servings.

SWEET BBQ PINEAPPLE

1	**fresh pineapple,** cored and sliced into $1/2$-inch-thick slices*
$1/2$ cup	**orange juice** or **apple juice**
$1/4$ cup	**brown sugar**
1 tablespoon	**cinnamon**
	vanilla ice cream

Combine all ingredients together and place in a shallow dish or large zipper-lock plastic bag. Marinate 1 hour or overnight; reserve marinade. Preheat grill to medium-high heat. Lightly oil grill. Grill pineapple slices 5–7 minutes per side, or until outside is dry and slightly charred. Serve warm with reserved marinade over vanilla ice cream. Makes 4–6 servings.

*Canned pineapple rings may be substituted.

KATHERINE'S SNAIL SNACKS

4	**slices white bread**
	butter
$^1/_4$ cup	**sugar**
I tablespoon	**cinnamon**

Mash bread flat, then butter one side. Mix sugar and cinnamon in a bowl. Sprinkle flattened and buttered bread with sugar mixture. Roll the bread, coating on the inside, into a tight roll. Grill 3–4 minutes over medium heat, turning every minute until light brown. Remove from grill and cut into $^1/_2$- to 1-inch pieces. Makes 2–4 servings.

Bonus Section: Sauces and Rubs

JAZZED-UP BBQ SAUCE

1 bottle (18 ounces) **BBQ sauce,** any variety
1/2 can **cola,** not diet
1/2 **sweet onion,** finely diced

Mix all ingredients together in a bowl. Remember, marinating meat in sauce at least 30 minutes before grilling gives meat a more robust flavor. Makes 2 cups.

STEVE'S FAMOUS DRY RUB

1/2 cup **white sugar**
1/2 cup **brown sugar**
1/4 cup **coarse salt**
2 tablespoons **freshly ground black pepper**
2 tablespoons **dried chopped onion**
1 tablespoon **paprika**
1 tablespoon **garlic salt**

Mix all ingredients together in a bowl. Use on your favorite meat about 60 minutes before grilling. Store any extra in an air-tight container, making sure to keep dry. Makes 1 1/2 cups.

FOUR-MINUTE BBQ SAUCE

1 cup **ketchup**
1/2 cup **brown sugar**
1/4 cup **mustard**
1/2 tablespoon **Worcestershire sauce**
1 tablespoon **vinegar**
1/2 teaspoon **ground ginger**

Mix all ingredients together in a bowl. Remember, marinating meat in sauce at least 30 minutes before grilling gives meat a more robust flavor. Makes 1 1/2 cups.

HONEY GARLIC BBQ SAUCE

1 bottle (18 ounces)	**honey BBQ sauce**
$1/2$ can	**cola,** not diet
$1/4$ cup	**honey**
1 to 2 tablespoons	**minced garlic**

Mix all ingredients together in a bowl. Remember, marinating meat in sauce at least 30 minutes before grilling gives meat a more robust flavor. Makes $2^1/2$ cups.

MOP SAUCE

1 cup	**cider vinegar**
2 tablespoons	**salt**
1 tablespoon	**brown sugar**
1 teaspoon	**minced garlic**
1 tablespoon	**dried chopped onion**
1 teaspoon	**horseradish** or **cayenne pepper**
$1/2$ cup	**cola** or **rootbeer,** not diet

Mix all ingredients together in a bowl. Remember, marinating meat in sauce at least 30 minutes before grilling gives meat a more robust flavor. Makes 2 cups.

BIG RED'S SPICY DRY RUB

$1/2$ cup	**freshly ground black pepper**
$1/2$ cup	**ground cayenne pepper**
1 cup	**dark brown sugar**
3 tablespoons	**salt**
1 teaspoon	**garlic powder**

Mix all ingredients together in a bowl. Use on your favorite meat 60 minutes before grilling. Store any extra in an air-tight container, making sure to keep dry. Makes $2^1/4$ cups.

ALABAMA WHITE BARBECUE SAUCE

1 cup **mayonnaise**
1/2 cup **vinegar** (preferably cider)
1 tablespoon **lemon juice**
1/4 to 1/2 teaspoon **horseradish** or **cayenne pepper**
1 teaspoon **minced garlic**
salt and pepper, to taste

Mix all ingredients together. It is best to refrigerate this sauce at least 8 hours before using, but it can be used immediately. Remember, marinating meat in sauce at least 30 minutes before grilling gives meat a more robust flavor. Makes 1 1/2 cups.

Set some aside for a great dipping sauce.

BRINE

1 cup **water**
1 tablespoon **Kosher salt**
1 tablespoon **sugar**

Mix all ingredients together. Makes 1 cup. If brining a lot of meat, make enough to cover completely.

SAUCE FROM SCRATCH

1/2 envelope **dry onion soup mix**
1/2 cup **brown sugar**
2 cups **ketchup**
1/2 teaspoon **Worcestershire sauce**
1 teaspoon **minced garlic**

Mix all ingredients together in a bowl. Remember, marinating meat in sauce at least 30 minutes before grilling gives meat a more robust flavor. Makes 2 1/4 cups.

FLOYD'S FANTASTIC SAUCE

¹/2 bottle **hickory smoke BBQ sauce** or **steak sauce**
I cup **Dr. Pepper**
¹/2 cup **ketchup**
2 tablespoons **lemon juice**
I tablespoon **cider vinegar**

Add some or all of the following:
I teaspoon **liquid smoke**
I tablespoon **Worcestershire sauce**
I tablespoon **salsa**
I tablespoon **minced garlic**
4 tablespoons **finely diced sweet onion**

Mix all ingredients together. It is best to refrigerate this sauce at least 8 hours before using, but it can be used immediately. Remember, marinating meat in sauce at least 30 minutes before grilling gives meat a more robust flavor. Makes 2¹/2 cups.

Set some aside for a great dipping sauce.

COACH'S ISLAND-STYLE MARINADE

¹/4 cup **soy sauce**
¹/4 cup **finely chopped green onions**
2 tablespoons **brown sugar**
2 tablespoons **sesame oil**
I tablespoon **minced garlic**
I tablespoon **toasted sesame seeds**

Mix all ingredients together in a bowl. Remember, marinating meat in sauce at least 30 minutes before grilling gives meat a more robust flavor. Makes I cup.

TEXAS BBQ SAUCE

3 cans (8 ounces each)	**tomato sauce**
$^1/_4$	**sweet onion,** finely minced
$^1/_2$ cup	**brown sugar**
$^1/_2$ teaspoon	**mustard powder**
I tablespoon	**honey**
$^1/_4$ teaspoon	**cayenne pepper**
I teaspoon	**minced garlic**
I to 2 teaspoons	**liquid smoke**

Mix all ingredients together in a saucepan, and simmer I hour. Remember, marinating meat in sauce at least 30 minutes before grilling gives meat a more robust flavor. Makes $3^1/_2$ cups.

HAWAIIAN GINGER MARINADE

$^1/_4$ cup	**sugar**
$^1/_4$ cup	**soy sauce**
$^1/_4$ cup	**oil**
$^1/_4$ cup	**water**
2 tablespoons	**molasses**
2 teaspoons	**minced garlic**
I teaspoon	**ginger**
I teaspoon	**dry mustard**
I teaspoon	**salt**

Combine all ingredients in a blender until smooth. Pour into a sealable container and store in refrigerator. Shake before using. Makes $1^1/_4$ cups.

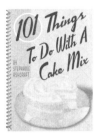

Yum! Each 128 pages, $9.95

Available at bookstores
or directly from GIBBS SMITH, PUBLISHER

1.800.748.5439

www.gibbs-smith.com

ABOUT THE AUTHOR

Steve Tillett is the king of backyard BBQ, and has done it all of his life. Growing up, he was even trained to BBQ, as he was the son of a butcher. A podiatric surgeon, Steve spent his post-graduate and medical residency training years in the South and Midwest, where his BBQ style flourished. Over the past couple of decades, he has created a group of recipes in his own backyard that are fun and delicious by any BBQ warrior's standard. Steve currently lives in Portland, Oregon, with his family. For more great information on BBQ, check out his web site www.bbq101.com.